NATIVE AMERICAN

In Harmony with Nature

Current Teachings from a Wise Ancient People

Kevin Kuzgan

Native Americans

in Harmony with Nature

Current Teachings from a Wise Ancient People

Kevin Kuzgan

Table of Contents

Introduction

Congratulations on purchasing *Native Americans in Harmony with Nature.*

The following chapters will discuss the history of Native Americans. Until recently, many history books used in school would note that America was discovered in 1492 by Christopher Columbus. Most of us remember growing up and having to memorize "in 1492, Columbus sailed the ocean blue." The truth was that by this time, people had been living on the continent for over 12,000, and they comprised culturally rich and varied societies. None of the Native American tribes were the same, and their languages, customs, and even ways of getting food were different, defined by the areas they settled in.

These tribes, each with their distinct language, religion, society, and way of life, had thrived for a long period of time, much longer than those seen in some of the other parts of the world. For example, Ancient Mesopotamia, which is known today as the cradle of civilization, spawned several important empires that then led to the development of medicine, art, and science as we know it today.

But by the time that many European settlers there started to create their city-states in the year 3,000 B.C., the people of the Americas had been living in their own settled societies for thousands of years. These great cultures of Europe, which arose in the first millennium of A.D., were short-lived when we compare them to what was going on in America. This is part of what makes the history of the Native Americans one of the greatest untold stories of all time.

When the European settlers did start to show up in America, the effect was cataclysmic for the people who were already living there. The new arrivals brought modern technology that, in some ways, helped the natives, but often, the diseases were enough to wipe most of them out and allowed the settlers to take over and do what they want.

Another thing that the Europeans brought with them was a viewpoint that said these native people, who were mostly peaceful, were savages who did not deserve the same time or consideration as what was given to civilized people. In a very short period of time societies and cultures that had been around and existing in harmony for thousands of years were obliterated and were replaced by the new settlers, who ended up disturbing the balance of nature and were able to wipe out a very large amount of the native people, often with very little regret and concern in the process.

This is what we are going to spend some time on in this guidebook. We are going to explore some more about the Native Americans, some of their societies, social norms, languages, religions, and the way that they interact with the world around them. We can learn so much from them, even after the storied past that we shared with them with the founding of America. We can learn so much from these people throughout the trials and tribulations that they have gone through, and that is what we will look at through this guidebook. Let's dive in and learn more about the story of the Native American people.

There are plenty of books on this subject on the market, thanks again for choosing this one! Every effort was made to ensure it is full of as much useful information as possible; please enjoy it!

Chapter 1: The Origin
Passing the Bering Straight

The first part of this that we need to explore is how the Native Americans originally got over to the American region. While these people had been in the area of North and South America for a long time, it is still believed that way back at the beginning of time. They started in the Mesopotamia area like the rest of civilization as well. While that theory makes sense for how people got to Africa, Asia, Europe, and so on, those were all connected and were relatively easy to traverse over a longer period of time.

What becomes a bit harder to work with here is how the Native Americans were able to get across the large Pacific, or even the large Atlantic if they went the other way to get to our present-day North and South America? The theory is that they crossed the Bering Sea.

The traditional story of human migration in the Americas includes a group of people moving from the area of Siberia to Alaska when the receding ocean waters were able to create a kind of land bridge, connecting the two continents in a manner that is not present today. Since it is a relatively short distance of land that we are talking about here, it makes sense that the waters may have gone back enough for people to cross on over.

Once across, the giant ice sheets of Cordilleran and Laurentide, which were able to block the area of southern Alaska and the Yukon Territory in western Canada, halted the progress of the migrants for some time. And that is the reason why we see some tribes still in that area as they chose to stay there rather than moving on.

Then, about 13,000 years ago, it is believed that these major ice sheets started to retreat, and in the process, they opened up about 900 miles of path that followed along the Rockies in Canada. This, according to many researchers, is how the Clovis culture was able to move down south over time, and slowly they were able to colonize many of the other parts of the Americas in the process.

Now, this is just the basics of how people would have gotten over. There are a number of reasons why those people may have gotten onto the Bering straight in the first place, and we have to remember that this is something that took place over a large number of years. These people may have needed more land as the world became more populated, and so moved north to find that. They may have followed the animals at the time to get enough food.

This was a process that took a good deal of time to accomplish, many thousands, and was not a mass exodus that got the people over and through America in a few years. As they went, many times some would be left behind happy with the new settlement. We can agree that there are still those Native American tribes found way up in Alaska around the edge, using fishing to help them gather the food that they want. They may be the descendants of the group who did not go further after crossing the Bering straight at the time.

There is also some new evidence that has added a bit of haziness to some of the timelines that we discussed above. There is some research that has come out, which shows us that humans were living further south of the ice sheets even before this ice-free corridor opened up. For example, there is a settlement found in Monte Verde, Chile, which shows that a group of people had made it all the way down to South America about 15,000 years ago, and there is even evidence that shows humans were hunting mammoths in Florida about 14,500 years ago.

Now, there is a newer study that is being done by an international team that is going to take a look at this ice hypothesis and see whether that is the way that the Native Americans actually made it to other parts of our world or not. With the help of sediment cores and some analysis of DNA, the researchers in this team were able to go through and reconstruct the environment that the corridor would have created. This kind of research shows that there just weren't enough resources in this pass for the human migrants to make it all the way through this as well.

The main thing that is a problem here is that even though this physical corridor is still believed to have opened about 13,000 years ago, it was going to be another few hundred years before it was possible to go through and use it. It is believed that because it took so long for this to open, and the limited number of resources found in the path (meaning people would have likely starved to death before getting through), there is now a theory that another route to get to other parts of America.

There are other theories that are out there that could be possible as well. Right now, researchers are taking a look at an area of the ice-free corridor that was once part of the large lake known as Glacial Lake Peace that may have blocked the path. It is believed that the migrants wouldn't be able to get across that water because it was 6,000 square miles, at least until it started to recede. This is something that we would be able to see in the sediment of the lake bed and with some of the remains of animals and plants if it did happen.

Today this is the area that is covered by Spring Lake in the Alberta region and Lake Charlie in British Columbia. The researchers on this team decided to take a visit to both of these lakes during the cold winter and then did some drilling down into the lake beds in order to get sediment cores and see what would happen.

Then they went through and used an effective technique known as shotgun sequencing to the materials they brought up. This works in allowing them to better date when the animals and plants would begin to colonize the lake bed. It is believed that the scraps they were able to get of DNA from all of this showed how for a time, Lake Peace receded, which would be a slow opening of that ice corridor. Birch, willow, and grasses would then begin to colonize the edges of the lake as it was shrinking and drying, and they found that about 12500 years ago, there was then evidence of jackrabbits and bison in the area as well.

While this could be a place that some native Americans came down, later on, dating is still not going to work. There may have been some resources and such, but not enough to keep the people alive, and they needed to work with a bit more. This is why it is believed that humans were most likely to follow the Pacific coast around these major ice sheets in order to make their way down to North and finally to South America.

This is still something that people need to study and learn more about as they go. The researchers need to spend some time focusing on what evidence they are able to find along the coast. This can be a bit harder to work with because of the tides and erosion and how this area is not going to be as preserved as it would near ice sheets and more. But it is something that could be done.

While there is still some debate out there about how long it took for the Native Americans to get down here, some saying not until about 13,000 years ago and some saying closer to 15,000 years and they were down in South America, and there is still some debate on what path they took. But what we know is that they did make it across the Bering straight at some point, and then, as the time when on and some of the paths became available, they were able to make their way on down through North America, and eventually onto South America.

We must remember that no matter which of the theories we are looking at here, the movement was slow and steady. It was not something that happened over a few years, and then everyone was stretched out. For some of the same reasons that they left the Mesopotamia area and got out of that into the north and then across the Bering Sea, these tribes would continue to move, finding their areas to settle in, and adapting their religion, language, and more based on that as well.

For example, some may have gone and followed the animals they were hunting. When the animals went east or south or somewhere else, they would follow and make that area their home. Some may have just stayed along the coast. Others may have liked being able to have more land to themselves and didn't want to be overcrowded, so they moved to get away when the area got too full.

No matter the reason, many tribes began to form in many areas of North and South America until they formed some of the areas that we know and are familiar with as well. While they may have had the same origins as each other, it is hard to find a tribe in one area that is the same as the other tribes. And that is part of what makes the native Americans so special and unique in their ways. They took the time to learn the land and figure out what was best for them in that particular area. They learned how to speak their languages and set up their customs, and they even learned how to build up their societies and trade with one another when another tribe was nearby. And all of this was done thousands of years before many of the other great civilizations of the world came into existence!

Chapter 2: The Allocation Living Along the Great Rivers and Following the Bison

It can be easy to regard those who settled into North and South America as just one single group of people, the Native Americans. The truth, though, is that all of these people developed their own ethnic, cultural and social groupings. They even had their social systems and languages based on where they settled. These groups, which were usually then divided up into tribes who would share a common language, were scattered all across this part of the world.

It is believed that up to ten million people in these tribes may have been in the Americas before the first white settlers even showed up. And the lifestyles of each tribe were going to differ based on their climate and landscape; those who lived in the colder northern regions would have different customs and languages and social norms compared to those who lived in the more temperate and warm climates to the south.

Even those who were in similar geographic areas were diverse and distinct from one another as well. Each group had their customs and ways of doing things, though we can certainly find some instances where they are similar to one another. To help us understand these people as a whole, even while understanding some of the differences that make them special and unique, we are going to take a look at the different regions they all settled in.

Arctic Region

This would be the area of present-day Canada and Alaska. The people here would live in both the semi-nomadic and hunter-gatherer groups and sometimes in some smaller villages. Two peoples inhabited these lands that are often considered inhospitable, the Aleut and the Inuit. The Inuit were considered nomads, living in small homes that were made out of animal skins and were portable. They often survived by hunting the polar bear and seals as they moved across the frozen landscape. The Aleut, on the other hand, had been comparatively more settled, and they were often found living in villages near the seas as they relied on fish and other seafood to keep them fed.

Subarctic Region

Then we are able to look at the subarctic groups. Much of inland Alaska and Canada were only slightly less inhospitable than the arctic that we just worked with. This area would have a large amount of taiga or snow forests with some waterlogged tundra and swamps that came with it. The population that was originally found in these lands and still found there was sparse and at least semi-nomadic.

People from these areas would like in some tents or eaves and would be able to survive by hunting large animals and hunting caribou. Sometimes they would follow this game and food as it migrated. There are two main ethnic groups who settled in this area, with the Athabaskan speakers in the east, which including the Cwich'in and the Tsattine tribes and then the Algonquian speakers in the west.

Northeast Coast

This is the region that is able to stretch from the Atlantic coast west to where our North Carolina is today and is sometimes counted as far as the Mississippi River Valley. This area is considered to be more temperate in a climate that allowed the tribes who stayed here to live a different type of life. In this area, the game was more plentiful, and the tribes did not need to migrate to find their food.

This is one area where settled villages were established, and some of these grew into some small towns with fortifications around them. The Algonquians of this area would settle in some of the coastal areas and would develop villages where they could become more adept at fishing. These groups also worked with agriculture as well, including beans, maize, and vegetables.

Plains

This is a vast area of open prairie and mountain that would stretch all the way from the Mississippi River Valley that we talked about earlier to the Rocky Mountains and from the U.S. Canada border all the way to the Gulf of Mexico, so you know that we are talking about a really big area here. The people who lived here were seen as hunters who were able to exploit the big herds of buffalo they shared the land with as food and for skins.

These people were settled for the most part and would live in some smaller villages as well. It was common for a lot of these people to become more nomadic as the white settlers joined the land, and many of the things that we associate with Native Americans today, including the tepees, war bonnets, and more, were found with this group of people. And most of these just came about when they had to change up their way of life to adapt to the new people on the land.

The Great Basin

This was a huge land that was barren and not hospitable to those who lived there, found between the Rocky Mountains and the Sierra Nevada on the east and west and then the Colorado Plateau and the Columbia Plateau to the other directions. Those tribes who lived in this area, which included the Ute and Pauite, were mostly nomadic in their way of life. They lived on foraging for berries and roots and would hunt small animals, lizards, and snakes for their food.

California

The land that is in the area we call California today was seen as one of the most densely populated parts of all North America before the arrival of the white settlers. However, this is going to be relative when we compare how sparsely the rest of the continent was populated at the time. It is estimated that, right before the arrival of the outsiders, this land alone had about 300,000 people who all belonged to a large number of unique tribes.

It is believed that at one time, there were 100 different tribes in this area, and they each had their unique languages between them. This group was more of a nomadic hunter-gatherer, and they would live in some small, portable, and temporary homes of skin and wood. There was not much agriculture going on in the area, but this network of tribes did bring in an extensive amount of trade between them.

The Plateau

The ad then we need to take a look at the area known as the Plateau, which was the area that was found in the basins of the Fraser and Columbia Rivers and is found between some of the other groups that we are talking about. It is an area of rolling hills and forests, and the people who lived here had smaller settlements that were close to the rivers. They would often survive on things like gathering up roots, nuts, and fruits and they liked to hunt and fish as well.

The Northwest Coast

This area is one that ran up the Pacific coast from California on the south side of it to the Canadian border in the north. It is an area with a pretty mild climate and a lot of natural resources for the people to use. The rivers of the area, as well as the whole coast of the region, were popular, and the tribes here were able to develop into towns as well. we are able to find a lot of social systems and complex hierarchies compared to some of the other groups of Native Americans.

Some of the towns that were found in this area were able to house hundreds of people, and social status was, at least in part, defined by possessions. This means that the more skins, canoes, and blankets that the person owned, the higher their position would be in the tribe. This was a big society that wasn't found in some of the other similar tribes at the time.

Southeast

The Southeast area is next, and it is found between the Gulf of Mexico and the Northeast. This was home of the "Five Civilized Tribes." These people would speak Muskogean and would include some of the groups that we may find familiar today, including the Creek, Muscogee, Chickasaw, Choctaw, and Cherokee. Later on, the Seminole would join them as well. This was a fertile area, and many of the people who lived in this area settled in villages and hamlets. For the most part, they were farmers who spent their time growing squash, beans, and maize.

Southwest

The last group that we are going to look at are those who are in the Southwest. This area is going to include where Arizona and New Mexico area today. The native people found in this area had two very unique ways of living. Some of the tribes, like the Yaqui and the Hopi, were farmers who grew things like squash, beans, and maize. These people made up their permanent villages that were adobe made. Other tribes that we are able to find in this area, including the Apache and the Navajo, lived more as nomadic gatherers and hunters, and their homes were often temporary and small, made out of mud and wood.

As we can see, while there are a number of different tribes that fall under the category of Native Americans, all of them developed their lifestyle and way of doing things that were different and unique. Sometimes this was based on their preferences and maybe where that group of people came from in the first place, but often it was influenced by what was around them and what resources they had available.

Chapter 3
Establishment of the United States
Birth of a Great Nation

For a long time, the people of this land were able to live and enjoy their lives. They had their customs and languages and ways of doing things, as we spent some time exploring above, but they also were able to live simple lives that were full and prosperous, and they got to enjoy all that the land was able to give to them. And then something happened that threw their way of life out the window and changed the way that they were going to live their lives from now on.

No one is quite sure who the first visitors from Europe to America were. It seems likely though that the Vikings were some of the first who arrived back during late tenth century A.D. Even though they were some of the first to make it here, they established settlements that were small and temporary, and they didn't make any attempts to come in and conquest the mainland that is found in America.

We are able to find some of the settlements of the Vikings in Canada, and it is thought that they had some motivation to head on down the east coast of this land in order to find some good timber for boat building and other types of construction. Though they may have been here for some time, it seems like the Vikings and their impact on the Native Americans were pretty minimal as well.

After the Vikings, the next explorers from Europe who arrived in the Americas came from the united kingdoms of Castile and Aragon, which are in the area we know as Spain today. These had emerged back in 1469 when Queen Isabella I from Castile married King Ferdinand II of Aragon. In the late fifteenth century, these kingdoms finally were able to complete the process known as the Reconquista, which ejected all of the Muslim forces from the southern part of Spain at the time. This allowed Catholic Spain to dominate that area.

Europe, for a long time up to this point, had been able to benefit from some good trading with the east, especially with the countries of India and China. However, the Ottoman Empire occupied Constantinople at this time, and this made it dangerous and difficult to continue with the trading. They didn't want it to stop though and many wondered if it were possible to reach Asia by sailing in the opposite direction.

One of those who believed that this was a possibility was Christopher Columbus, and in 1492, he convinced Queen Isabella to fund his expedition to sail across the Atlantic Ocean in order to find his new route to Asia. Then, after about a month after sailing out, the ships that Columbus was leading sighted land, most likely near the Bahamas or the Caicos or Turks Islands. Columbus initially thought that he had found the eastern side of Asia, which is why the people were then called Indians, but it didn't take long before the sailor realized that he was on a new continent.

It was during this time that Columbus started to explore more of the Caribbean and some of the northern parts of South America. Soon, word of his discovery spread, and then ships from a variety of other nations would start to follow. Just five years later, John Cabot, an explorer from Italy, would be able to find Newfoundland for the English crown. With these discoveries, the lives of the Native American tribes that were around would start to change in a dramatic manner.

Soon Spain was then able to establish some of the control that they wanted over the Caribbean area and some of South America as well. Initially, the Spanish people were friendly to the indigenous people there, trading and bringing with them a lot of novel and new items from Europe. This did not last too long, though, because the trade would then turn into conquest instead. The military forces in Spain had a lot more weaponry than the native people and soon, some of the biggest empires of the area, the Inca and Aztecs, were brought under the control of Spain.

In addition to bringing some of their new items and technology to the New World with them, the Spanish people brought many diseases, including measles, typhus, and smallpox Since the native people had no immunity to this, they were wiped out within a short amount of time. It was estimated that the local populations were decreased by 80 percent by the time 1548 came around. And by 1580, around half of those who survived the diseases were killed when a new epidemic started. This was one of the reasons why it was so easy for Spain to gain the firm control that they wanted over these new colonies, and they were able to hold it for another 300 years.

Now, the conquest that happened in North America took a bit more time. This was mainly because the continent lacked the silver and gold that South America had. The Spanish colonists, with the help of Hernando de Soto, occupied the area of present-day Florida, and they moved up north. One of the first battles that happened between the native people and Europeans occurred in 1540 in October. This was when the de Soto forces attacked the town of Mabila.

The technology that the native people had at the time was no match for all of the newer weapons that were found in Europe. During this battle, those in de Soto's army only had 22 dies while the Native Americans in the hat area lost more than 2500 people. And this would soon change to a big pattern each time that the natives tried to fight anyone from Europe.

During this time, the French were also able to establish some small colonies in North America in the sixteenth century. But these did not last for a long time. It was about 100 years after the Spanish first started in the Americas before other powers in Europe would start to colonize and work more in North America. The French were able to establish some of the first settlements that were permanent in the area of Canada during the earlier years of the seventeenth century. The English followed with some of their settlements in Plymouth and Jamestown, to name a few.

In the beginning, these were just used as posts for trading. Private companies were able to operate these to make money and send things back to their home countries rather than these being sponsored and ran by the governments of those countries. Contact with the Native Americans during this time was pretty much peaceful, and many of these groups were willing to trade some of the furs they got for other items and goods that were in Europe.

It didn't take long before both the English and the French governments decided that they needed to have some control over these colonies rather than letting them do whatever they want. To start, the French declared the existence of New France, which was going to be a large area that had five colonies going from the Gulf of Mexico to the Hudson Bay and out to the Great Lakes area. And then the English followed by having some royal charters to create some formal counties in the area which is now known as New England.

Just like we were able to see in the South America area, the arrival of more Europeans in North America also brought about a lot of diseases that proved to be lethal to the native people. For example, it is estimated that around the Massachusetts Bay area, about 90 percent of the native people were killed by smallpox during that time. This made it a lot easier for these countries to go in and take over the areas, and often they were able to do it without any direct conflicts with the people who originally lived there. It is believed that these diseases caused a massive amount of death at the time, and it ended up breaking up and disrupting the culture and societies of the Native Americans.

Many of the earlier settlers of this area would enlist the native people to fight on their behalf, and they would look for some of the enmities that were already there between the tribes to help them out with this. The French settlers found themselves being allied with the Huron tribe, who had hated the Iroquois for a long time. The French would supply firearms to the Huron and they were then able to rout out these foes and expand the area of control that they had.

Of course, the Iroquois would be able to fight back, and they worked to create a confederacy of smaller tribes who would fight against the French and the Huron. The French had to occupy the homeland of the Iroquois for a bit, though this only brought on peace for a short amount of time. After about 50 years of this kind of conflict, it was only concern about the expansion of the colonies of England, which started to get into this area, which persuaded the Iroquois and the French to make peace and then ally together to fight the English.

The colonists of England also had some threats from other tribes in the area. King Philip's War, which is also called the First Indian War, was a series of conflicts that happened between the English and their allies of native people against the Narragansett and Wampanoag tribes. This conflict lasted for three years from 1675 to 1678 only ended because the two tribes that fought against the English were almost destroyed.

This also caused a lot of damage to the colonies at the time, and there were several towns that were destroyed, and one in ten men who were old enough to fight had died. The fact that England had not provided any support to their colonists during these three years led many to wonder whether the colonies would be better off without being a part of England, and may have been some of the beginning thoughts for the American Revolution that would come up later on.

The beginning history that we are able to see between the colonists and the native tribes was to outline how their relations would go for a long time. Some would come in ready to fight and take over the trusting natives who had no immunity against some horrible diseases. And others would be friendly for as long as it took at the time, and once it benefited them more to turn, they would start to fight and take over. This would end with many wars and bloodshed, with a lot of changes to the way of life for the native people as well.

Chapter 4
Expansion to the West
To Conquer the West

Many of us already know a lot about some of the western expansion of the North American land. Many of our states are due to this, and we know that the Europeans were not happy to just stay by the coastline in order to make all of this happen. Think about how different our world would be if they were just willing to stay in the New England area and not expand out. But the same kind of greed and more that allowed them to take over the New World and fight the natives at that time was the same drive that moved many English and other Europeans to push on into America and take more and more.

By the mid-1700s, there were three main European countries who had been able to establish colonies in North America. The first one was Britain, was the largest because it had six colonies at the time where are mostly found in the area of New England today. They also had about 2 million settlers in this area. There was also France with colonies in the northwest and around the area of Newfoundland, but they only had about 60000 people at the time. And then Spain had some area in Florida, but the Empire was starting to weaken, and they never had more than a few hundred people in that area after that time.

The lives of those natives who were in the areas that France and Britain controlled became a lot different than what they were used to before these people arrived. Many of the tribes spent their time trading with the newcomers, which may have seemed like a good idea, but it was harmful in the way that it changed their lives.

One of the major issues that showed up here was that of alcoholism. Before the Europeans arrived, the Native American tribes didn't have a lot of contact with this kind of substance. Some of the southwester tribes of the time would brew wines and beers, but when compared to what the Europeans brought, these had really low levels of alcohol and were reserved just to use during religious ceremonies of the time. When the Europeans came, they brought distilled spirits that were a lot strong, as well as some brand new attitudes about alcohol.

Most of the Europeans at this time were pretty suspicious about drinking water because many of their cities did not have a good sanitation present. This led to many of them feeling that alcoholic beverages, no matter the kind, were a lot safer to drink than the water. The settlers were able to make wines from fruits and vegetables and then cider from apples. And at the time, the most popular alcoholic beverage would be rum. It wasn't long before this rum became an important feature for them to use when dealing with the native people.

Often traders would trade some of the cheaply produced local beer and rum in order to get some pelts and skins. They also found it beneficial to pass around the rum when they were doing negotiations, knowing full well that the native people were not all that used to the alcohol and would get intoxicated quickly. This quickly wore down some of the social structures that had been in place with these tribes for thousands of years, and many of the people became addicted to the spirits that the traders gave to them.

Back in Europe, there were a lot of people who thought that a major conflict was about to happen. The continent had been split into two opposing confederations. There was Great Britain, which led a group of countries, including Prussia,

Portugal, and some other small nations, while France started to head a group that had Russia, Austria, and Span. These two super-powers were in competition to gain control over Europe and the other colonies of the world at the time. The spark, which would turn this into a conflagration, came from America when George Washington, a young major in the British army, led forces to make an attack on France.

There had already been a few skirmishes that happened between these two powers, and often there was a lot of support from the Native Americans as well. While there was a lot of fighting on both sides of this, and some native people joined in with the French, it was found that many of these tribes decided to side with the British. For many, this was seen to be a pragmatic decision that was based on the idea that they traded with ad depended on the British more. For others, the fear of expanding colonies fostered a kind of belief that if they worked with the British, then the British would be able to stop some of the expansion.

Even though the Native Americans fought with the British, and even helped in part to win the American Revolution, it was quickly clear that these people would not be given the same rights and privileges as those who were white. The pursuit of happiness, liberty, and life was something that would only apply to those of power, and with white skin, and not to the others they saw as savages. And the British concurred with this when they signed the Treaty of Paris in 1783 because there were no representatives of the tribes who helped out both sides of the war.

Despite the fact that their way of life was being taken advantage of, and the fact that they had helped to win a war that was going to bring out a new country in the process the Native Americans were still struggling with a lot of the freedoms that they should have, and they were still seen as a lower people. This was just the start, though, and the time for the Natives would end up a lot bloodier and harder in the process.

Expanding America

After the Revolutionary War was done, there were a lot of bloody and frequent battles that happened between the Native Americans and the Americans. Many of these were on a smaller scale, including times when the native people would try to defend their lands against the white people moving in and taking them over. This situation was made even worse when government representatives and British agents, tried to get into this by adding guns to the arsenals of the native people, in the hopes that the Americans would not be able to expand out to the West.

Many of the conflicts that did occur were focused close to the Northwest Territory, an area that had been ceded to the Americans by the British after the war, without any reference to the people who were already living there at the time. Of course, there were some of these conflicts that were a lot larger in scale as well. For example, the Cherokee-American Wars, which began in part, during the Revolutionary war and then continued into the 1790s, often had bands with hundreds of warriors who would attack towns and villages.

In 1794, this war was ended thanks to the Treaty of Tellico Blockhouse, and the Cherokee were forced to cede over a large amount of their territory. The expansion of the colonies, even with some of these skirmishes, continued relentlessly, which caused a lot more conflicts with the Native Americans who tried to defend their homes and their ways of life.

There was very little objection to this take-over of the lands owned by the Native Americans by Americans or people elsewhere. Thanks to a lot of the propaganda and more that was going around about these people, most people thought the natives were savages, and that the whites had an obligation to take these lands and subject them to the benefits that civilization was able to give them.

In fact, during 1823, the Supreme Court in the United States gave a ruling that said that while the native people were allowed to live in their traditional homelands, they would not be the title holders to these lands. This then led to a new act known as the Indian Removal Act, which was passed in 1830 by Congress. This was the act that would make it legal for the president to eject the native people from their tribal lands if it were necessary.

Thanks to some of these new laws, the government was able to start their work in moving all of the native people from the southeast. For example, the Seminole tribes of Florida were moved over to Oklahoma, and large numbers of the Cherokee tribe were moved from Georgia to Oklahoma as well. This removal was not easy at all, and often, it was done with a lot of brutality and more for these people. Around 4000 of the Cherokee during these relocations died of starvation and disease, which resulted in the trek being known as the Trail of Tears.

The forced relocation of the Native Americans to new lands that seemed to be perfect for getting them out of the way meant that they were in places where they had no historical connections. These lands were also really barren and forgotten, and there were no ways for the people to do well with farming, hunting, or living. Because of this, there were still lots of conflicts and some wars that showed up. No matter how hard the native people tried though, they were no match for the numbers and the technology of the American people.

For most of these battles, the Native Americans were defeated by the military forces. Most of the tribes were small, did not have the military weapons of the Americans, and not as organized, and so they didn't stand much of a chance. As the white settlers stared to expand more of their control from east to west in America, it didn't take long before the native people were forced out of their lands, and often they were just killed instead.

In California, one tribe of indigenous people we were peaceful were completely decimated. Many militia units started to have a shoot on sight kind of policy towards these people instead of even trying to move them. This got to the point that in a 26 year period from 1850 onward, the native population in that area went from 150,000 to fewer than 30,000 people. These killings were not just random things with the military people in charge of going out of control. They were completely sanctioned by both the federal and the state governments, and the state government of Dakota in 1862 offered a reward of $200 for each native who was killed.

Then came Ulysses S. Grant. He became the president of the United States in 1869, and one of the first things he did in this role was to appoint General William Tecumseh Sherman as the commander of the army. The year before, Sherman had written a note to Grant, noticing that they needed to act in a vindictive way to the Sioux, even to exterminate the whole tribe. And it seemed like many

Americans agreed with eradicating the natives rather than working with them.

The Battle of Little Bighorn

Of course, the native people did win in some cases. There are a lot of little and big battles that occurred throughout the time of expansion by the white settlers, and being able to cover them all is going to be a challenge. But one battle, in particular, can show us how hard and valiantly the native people tried to fight in order to keep the Americans out of their land, and it shows us that they could, in some cases, get together and see success.

In June of 1876, General George Custer led part of the 7th Cavalry into the Lakota Sioux lands near the area of the Little Bighorn River. There was a battle that came about during this time, and during it, about five of the twelve regiments of the cavalry were wiped out. Along with this, Custer and his two brothers were killed in the fight.

This was a great win for the Native people. But it was a very isolated and unusual defeat because the forces of the U.S. government and most large engagements ended up leading to the defeat of those on the native side who tried to fight. There is some speculation that if the native people had been able to work together and fight against the military to win, then they may have had a chance. But there were just too many tribes spread out too much, and they had too many languages and customs. By the time they may have thought about joining together, it was too little too late, and not enough fighters left in order to handle this.

The impact of the white people on the populations of the natives was not just caused by these direct conflicts, though this did cut down on the number of people on the native sides. It was also brought on by some new methods and processes as well. for example, logging meant that a lot of the forests that the native people relied on for their food in hunting started to disappear.

The building of the new railroads throughout the United States was able to open up some new areas of exploitation as well. the herd of buffalo, which had once been limitless and all over the place, were taken out. In 1850, it was estimated that there were 60 million of these animals. But thanks to the railroad bringing out big parties of hunters who did not appreciate the land and the animal and who would just slaughter the animals, it was believed that by 1900, there were only 300 of these animals left.

The tribes who had relied on the buffalo for their food, shelter, clothes, and more, we're left with nothing. And in the plains, there wasn't much for them to replace it with. These people quickly started to die out, as well.

By the end of the nineteenth century, there was a lot of serious trouble for the indigenous people. Their numbers were depleted by quite a bit, and they had very little they could do to resist the government. They tried to fight again with the Wounded Knee, but they were taken over, and many of their women and children were killed in this as well. even the newspapers in America shortly after called this a bloodthirsty and wanton massacre. It wasn't until this time when the American people started to wonder about the actions they were taking against the native people, but still many things like reservations and more stuck around.

The massacre at Wounded Knee was seen as the last of the big confrontations between the native people and the U.S. army. By this time, the population of America was at more than 70 million people, and there were fewer than 250,000 native people combined left, and most of these were in the reservations, disarmed and disheartened as well. after this time, the native people would no longer pose a big threat to the people of America, and they were allowed to expand and spread out as much as they wanted.

The Propaganda Against Native Americans

It was the propaganda against these people, which allowed for many of these fights to occur in the first place. We can look back now and think about how the government treated the native people and wonder why they would act in this manner to start with. But at the time, most of the American people were all for these killings and the relocation of the native people.

The reason for this is that most of the American people believed that the natives were unfriendly and savages. Some may have seen it as their duty to go in and take control over the natives, maybe seeing it as their duty to teach them Christian religion in order to convert them and bring them over to the side of civilization at the time.

The fact that some of the native people had gone and started to fight against the whites, and some got to the point of going after women and children as well in the hopes of getting their land back, such as the Cherokees during the Revolutionary War, could have caused some problems. The newspapers were able to sensationalize the issue and make it seem that all of the native people would behave that way, making it even more prudent to get them out of the way and not have the American people harmed.

Considering that most native people during this time were sent to reservations and kept away from the American people, there was very little contact between them outside of the battles that usually went against the favor of the native people. It is hard to better understand people and their way of life if the only place you know anything about them is from the newspapers and never from any personal contact that you may have with them.

As sad as it may seem at the time, the American people believed that this was the best way for them to go through and keep themselves safe as well. They thought that this was the best way to keep themselves and their families safe, and many of them were just fine with the natives getting killed or at least getting put out of the way to not harm them in the process. It may not have been the right course of action, but it is the one that was able to shape the way that America is today.

Chapter 5: Indian Celebrity Legendary Stories of Brave Warriors

There were many brave warriors who came out in order to fight against the take over of their land, and the forcing of the native people to be on the reservations and away from their home. While many different tribes were taken over, and overall, we know that the Indian tribes did not win much, there were still a lot of valiant celebrities and brave warriors who took on the fight. Sometimes they won some small battles that showed their strength, even if the U.S. Army and government seemed to be way overpowering these groups along the way. Some of the well-known Native American warriors that we need to spend some time on includes:

Sitting Bull

The first person that we are going to take a look at is Sitting Bull. This chief is a Teton Dakotan who united a lot of the Sioux Tribes of the area in order to try and fight against the white settlers who were trying to steal from them and kick them out. The 1868 Fort Laramie Treaty granted some of the Black Hills lands to this group, who saw it as sacred. But as soon as gold was found in that treaty was ignored and the tribes were taken advantage of.

The Great Sioux Wars that came after this were then culminated in the 1876 Battle of Little Big Horn, where both Crazy Horse and Sitting Bull worked to lead tribes of Sioux who were united in the victory against Custer. It was in 1890 when Sitting Bull was shot, and that shot was enough to kill him. But this was still enough to remember him for his courage in defending the native lands.

Sitting Bull was born in 1831, close to the Dakota Territory in the South Dakota area. He was the son of Returns Again, who was a great Sioux warrior. The young boy killed his first buffalo when he was just 10, and by the time he was 14, he was joining in on some of the raids that were happening against the Crow camp. And this is when he was given his new name of Sitting Bull.

It wasn't long before he was able to join in with the Strong Heart warrior society as well as the Silent Eaters. Both of these groups were there to make sure that the tribe was doing well. he also worked to help expand out some of the hunting grounds of the Sioux into the west, fighting against other tribes, like the Crow, in order to get it.

It was in 1863 when Sitting Bull started to battle the U.S. Army. This happened when they were coming after the Santee Sioux because they wanted to retaliate for the Minnesota Uprising. There were more than 300 people from the Sioux tribe who ended up being arrested from this uprising, but President Lincoln commuted these sentences, and only 39 of the accused were kept.

Sitting Bull faced the might of the U.S. military when it was the Battle of Killdeer Mountain back in 1864, when the forces from the United States surrounded one of the trading villages, eventually forcing the Sioux who were in there to retreat. These scuffles were enough to convince Sitting Bull to never sign a treaty at all with the government and to never force his people to go onto the reservation.

Sitting Bull was instrumental in a lot of the Sioux tribe coming together and trying to defeat the American military and keep off the reservation. In many other parts, the native people would work on their own, and as many of their tribes were small, it was easier to be taken over, and the white settlers were able to get what they want without much trouble.

On the other hand, Sitting Bull joined together with other native tribes in that area in order to fight together. The numbers were still not big enough to overtake all of the power of the United States Army, but it was a much bigger challenge than what had come up before, and they were able to get some great results in the process as well.

Crazy Horse

Crazy Horse was born in 1841 in the Black Hills area of South Dakota. He was the son of the Oglala Sioux shaman of the same name, and his mother was one of the members of the Brule Sioux tribe. Crazy Horse had a complexion that was lighter than some of the others in his tribe, along with curls. It wasn't until he finished up a battle in 1858 with Arapaho warriors that he was given the name of his father, and then his father took on a new name.

In many different ways, Crazy Horse was not a traditionalist with regard to some of the customs of his tribe, and it wasn't uncommon for him to shrug off a lot of the different kinds of traditions as well as the rituals that were found with the people of the Sioux For example, Crazy Horse decided to go through and ride in the prairie during 1854 to get his vision quest, but he did not go along and complete some of the required rituals before starting. After he was out there and fasted for a total of two days, he had his first vision. During this, there was a horseman who came in and told Crazy Horse that he should go out into war without any adornments on himself. He was not allowed to have more than one feather at a time, and it was not allowed, according to this vision, for him to wear one of the war bonnets.

In 1866, there was gold discovered on the Bozeman Trail in the area of Montana. Many militaries worked to build up quite a few of their forts inside of the territory of the Sioux. Under the help of Captain Fetterman here, there was a U.S. troop who clashed with these warriors, and it was Crazy Horse who ended up being one of the decoys. His goal was to take 80 of the soldiers up to an ambush. The bodies were all hacked up in order to send back a strong message to Sherman.

In 1867, Crazy Horse was then able to take part in an attack on one of the smaller forts nearby. After this time, Sherman started to do a tour of these prairie lands to meet with the leaders and see if there is a way to seek out peace. By 1868, soldiers were pulled out of the forts, and then a treaty was signed that would give some of the native people back their ownership of the Black Hills area. Crazy Horse decided to avoid this treaty, though because he wanted to do the raids on these tribes instead.

Then it was during the time of 1872 when Crazy Horse entered into a raid along with Sitting Bull. This was a raid that was going against up to 400 Soldiers of America. It was during this time when Crazy Horse had his own horse shot while he was riding it, and instead of giving up, he got off and ran right to the army. Then later on, in 1873, He crossed paths with Custer again when Custer came back into the territory. It was near the Yellowstone River where the two came across each other. The Sioux tried to steal the horses of the sleeping soldiers, but there was a scuffle, and he then retreated with everyone else.

Then there was the Battle of Rosebud that happened in 1876. This was when a large number of tribes decided to gather in Montana in order to join with Sitting Bull. At this time, General George Crook, who had been trying to raid into a village that he thought was Crazy Horse's (which it wasn't), tried to attack, but Sitting Bull and Crazy Horse and led the forces to push back here.

Then a week later, General Custer entered into a battle that is known as the Little Big Horn after refusing to listen to the advice that some of his guides. These guides assured him that he would lose out when he tried to do this. At this time, about 1000 warriors, with the help of Crazy Horse, flank the forces of Custer and to help seal up the defeat of the general, and this became Custer's Last Stand in the process.

Crazy Horse was not done there. He then traveled on to Big Butte in order to harass some of the miners that were in this area, while the rest of the Sioux continued to face some of the issues and hostilities that General Crook was handling to them, but the winter was heard on the tribe, and not much happened. Sensing that the tribe struggling for survival at this part, Colonel Nelson Miles tried to come up with a deal working with Crazy Horse with the promise of helping out the Sioux this time.

When Crazy Horse decided to work with the emissaries in order to discuss how this deal would work, the soldiers shot and killed several of them, and Crazy Horse fled. Miles kept up the attack on the encampment until the winter got bad enough that they were not able to do it anymore. With the winter not going well, Crazy Horse negotiated with Lieutenant Clark, who offered the Sioux their reservation in exchange for their surrender, and Crazy Horse decided to work with them and take it.

Geronimo

Geronimo was a leader of the Apache tribe, as well as a medicine man best known for trying to resist anyone who was trying to remove his people out of their tribal lands. This includes both Americans and Mexicans. He repeatedly was able to evade the capture and life on a reservation, and during the final escape, there was estimated to be a full quarter of the U.S. standing army pursued him and his followers. When he was finally captured in September of 1886, he was the last leader of the Native Americans to formally surrender to the military. Then he spent the last twenty years of his life as one of the prisoners of war at the time.

Geronimo was born in the area of Arizona in 1829. His birth name was Goyahkla, or "one who yawns" and he was considered one of the sections of the Apache tribes, a small but mighty group altogether who had about 8000 people. By the time he was of age, the Apaches were already at war, fighting to the South with the Mexicans and then to the north with the U.s government, and with a few other native tribes as well. it was early on that he showed promise as a hunter, and he was able to lead four raids that were successful by the time he was 17.

It was a personal tragedy that ended up shaping his hatred for anyone who wanted to subject him and his people during that time. While he was on a trading trip in 1851, Mexican soldiers came in and attacked his family's camp. Geronimo's wife and their three children, along with his mother, were all murdered.

Full of all this grief, Geronimo burned the belongings of his family based on the traditions of the Apache before he went into the forest. During this time, he heard a voice that told him that a gun would not kill him and that his arrows would be guided to help him win the victory. He was soon able to hunt down the killers of his family and then devoted his life to avenging them.

The westward expansion of America brought a lot of new woes and foes to those in the Apache tribe. With the 1848 signing of the Treaty of Guadalupe Hidalgo, the end of the Mexican American War happened. Mexico then gave up much of the Southwest of America to the United States, including the land that the Apaches had been living in for a long time. And then the Gadsden Purchase that happened in 1854 made this even worse.

It was then in 1872 that the U.S. government created a reservation for the Apaches, and this included some of their homelands. But it did not take long before they were evicted and then forced to go in and join some of the other Apache tribes who were found in Arizona at the San Carlos Reservation. Geronimo, who was very defiant by that time, broke out of this reservation, along with some followers, three different times. Since he knew the land well, it was easier to evade his pursuers as well.

The more that Geronimo ran off and the longer that he was able to hide, the more it ended up embarrassing the government. His belief that no bullet was going to harm him appeared to be pretty much true because he was able to escape all of the skirmish's hats came up. While he did get harmed in some cases, he always recovered, and it wasn't long before he was a newspaper sensation.

In May of 1885, Geronimo led 135 of his followers to get away from the reservation yet again. To avoid capture again by the scouts and the cavalry that was watching for him, he often pushed the people who were in his group to go as much as 70 miles in a single day. While he was on the loose, Geronimo and those with him would raid settlements along the way, whether they were American or Mexican, and sometimes they killed civilians as well.

In March of 1886, General George Crook was able to force Geronimo to surrender, but then he and about 40 of his followers were able to leave and get out at the last minute. Then about 5000 soldiers from America and another 3000 Mexicans pursued him. They were able to hide out for another five months before Geronimo turned himself in September 1886.

When he turned himself in, he was taken over to Fort Pickens in Florida by train and then to the Mount Vernon Barracks in Alabama. He was eventually imprisoned in the Kiowa and Comanche reservations in the area of Oklahoma as well. Geronimo spent about 14 years here, leaving for just a few trips that were approved by the government, but usually, these included places where he was put on display as proof of the power of the government. He eventually died at Fort Sill on February 17, 1909.

Standing Bear

When Lewis and Clark spent years going westward in 1804, they heard about the Ponca, a small tribe that was living on the west bank of the Missouri River and the lower Niobrara River area. While the explorers did not meet the Ponca at this time because the group was out hunting to the west a bit, this was still an important tribe to consider at the time.

Standing Bear is believed to have been born around 1829 in the traditional Ponca Homeland that was near the Missouri and Niobrara rivers. About 30 years later, the tribe had to sell its homeland over to the U.S. government but were able to hold onto about 58000-acre reservations that happened between the Niobrara River and Ponca Creek. During this time on the reservation, the Poncas were able to live by farming, but often they were in fear because they did not get a lot of protection from the Sioux who lived nearby.

When the federal government created a new reservation for the Great Sioux in 1868, the Ponca Reservation was included in the boundaries of this new reservation. This left the Ponca with very little of their remaining lands to live on. Then in 1877, the federal government decided that it was time for the Poncas to be taken out to the Indian Territory. Standing Bear, the chief at that time, protested this eviction. This caused federal troops to remove them, and the result was that that the Poncas arrived in the Indian Territory during 1878.

The Poncas were in a new land with strangers, in the middle of a really hot summer, and they did not have any crops or prospects for planting them because they were there long past the time to do this. Since the tribe had been taken out of Nebraska, about one-third had died, and most of those who were left were disabled and sick. There was some talk at that time about having it done in the north in their old lands.

Then it happened in 1878 that some events set them in motion to go back home. When Standing Bear lost his son, he decided that it was time to go back home, and this was enough to bring back some fame and justice to these people. At the time his son died, Standing Bear wanted to honor the last wishes and bury him in the land of his birth, rather than in the strand country where it was believed his spirit would just wander around forever. It was a few members of the tribe along with Standing Bear, many of whom were women and children, who headed on back to the homeland of the Poncas, which was north of this time.

It was sometime in January when this band headed on through the whole of what is known as the Great Plains, and it was not a fun journey or them. They took two months before they were able to meet up with the Omaha tribe, who were their relatives. During this time, Standing Bear was able to carry the bones of his son, and the goal was to bury these right on the Niobrara River.

Because none of the Indians were allowed to go out of the reservations without permission, Standing Bear and the ones who went with him were considered a renegade band. The Army took this band and arrested them before keeping all of them at Fort Omaha. The idea at the time was to bring them back to what was known as the Indian Territory. They got a little reprieve here because General George Crook had some sympathy for the cause and what Standing Bear was doing, and he employed the help of Thomas Tibbles, a newspaper man in the area, to help out. Tibbles took this case and secured two attorneys in Omaha to help represent Standing Bear.

The lawyer filed an application in federal court for a write of habeas corpus to test whether there was any legality in the detention, basing their case on the 14th Amendment. The government then disputed the right of Standing Bear to be able to obtain this in the first place because it did not see an Indian as a "person' under this kind of law. However, the Judge of this case ruled in favor of Standing Bear because they saw that Standing Bear, and those who followed him, were indeed considered "people" under the law, and they were entitled to be free to enjoy the rights that anyone else in the land did.

The government did decide to try and appeal the decision that was made here. But at the time, the Supreme Court refused to even hear the case. This left Standing Bear and his followers to be free based on the law and opened up the door to see other Native Americans of the time more as people, rather than savages, something they had not been able to enjoy before.

Chapter 6: Cultural Aspects
Myths, Soul, Legends
Art, Wit and Wisdom
of American Indians

Now that we know a bit about the beginnings of this people, and all that they went through to develop their own cultures and then the taking over of their lands and society that the white settlers did, it is time to learn a bit more about the people we are looking at. We have some of the background information, and some of that can serve us well as we go along. But we need to also focus more on how they lived their lives, the things that were important to them, and more. We are going to spend some of our time in this chapter looking at more of the cultural aspects of this group of people, their art, myths, legends, and more so that we can learn from this amazing group of people.

Spirituality

The first thing that we will look at here includes some of the rituals and ceremonies of the Native American people. Keep in mind that all of the tribes were very diverse, and there were variations of these throughout time as well. we are going to take a look at some of the basics of these and some of the general parts that seem to be found among the tribes that are similar.

It isn't too hard to see some of the depth in the spirituality that these people had when we simply look at some of their craftworks. This spirituality of the native tribes included a strong reverence for the environment around them, for the lives of animals, and one another as well.

The spirituality of the natives is not going to be the same as what we see as the religion for other people. These tribes did not have religious meetings that were organized, and history shows that, at least in the beginning, this was more of a way they lived their life rather than a religion as we see it today.

One thing that we will find a bit different from the native tribes is that they have a kind of reverential use of tobacco thanks to the white man bringing it in. And while alcohol was not originally a part of this process, it has slowly come in and taken over even some of the religion of the native people as well.

As we mentioned, each tribe has some different rules and traditions that they will follow when it comes to this spirituality. Most of them had some kind of ritual in place that would represent the hunt, and for growing produce, for them to eat. Since this was the main source of food for these tribes, following the right rituals was imperative to how well the tribe would do. Many of these tribes would have a variety of rituals and ceremonies that they would practice before, and often after, a big hunting expedition. They believed that these rituals would help them to be successful on the hunt.

In addition, history shows that when the white men came to the various tribes, they saw the traditions and rituals as a bunch of superstitions and old tales that would not hold up to the religion that most of the white man was following at the time. Because of this, many of the leaders of a tribe would spend up to 30 years in jail due to their traditions and customers. In many cases, the governments in Canada and the United States tried to force the native people to change the way that they practiced their religion, usually forcing them into religions, like Christianity, that was seen as more suitable.

History also shows us that there were many tribes that had special leaders known as Shamans. The Shaman was the one who would be responsible for overseeing this spirituality for the tribe in order to make sure they were doing it right, that they were going to see success after performing the rituals and more

The belief was that spirits were able to enter into the body of the Shaman during their ceremonies, and when they chanted and beat on the drums, this whole process would be successful. This is why many people of the tribe would believe that the Shamon was truly able to tell them why a hunting trip did not turn out in the successful manner they wanted, or why some people were being afflicted with an illness in the camp.

Many tribes also believed that there were spirit creatures around them as well. For example, they believed that these creatures were able to control the weather. This is why we see traditions of the rain dance, along with some other rituals, in order to help out during draughts and more.

Depending on the tribe we take a look at here, there are some tribes that believe that all animals around them were originally human and that the people in that tribe would share the same ancestors from long ago with these animals. Even for the tribes that did not believe animals were originally human, there was a high respect for animals as part of the land, and these tribes practiced only using what they needed, not killing animals for fun, and respecting the world around them.

When young boys reached the age of puberty in their tribes, they would go outside into the wilderness, leaving the camp behind. During their time away from the camp, they would receive a vision that was meant to help guide them as they finished out their years into adulthood and through the rest of their lives as well. Each boy would have a different vision they would receive from the spirits. Females would not join this part of the religion.

Then there was a special part of these beliefs that was known as the Sundance. This was a ritual that was used to help pray for continual life, both for the humans of the tribe and for the bounty of the earth. This was also a good ritual to bring out good health, could build up a friendship with some of the surrounding tribes, and can help to thank the creator who was watching over them all.

The Myths

Now it is time for us to take a look at some of the myths that are available with the Native Americans, and we will start with some of the different creation myths since these can show us more about these people and their connection with the world.

The Apache

First are the Apache. This group has more than one myth about creation, and they will both contain animals and gods, and we will talk about both of them here. In the first myth, it is believed that two gods, Quetzalcoatl and Tepeu, thought everything into being. The tribes believe that the thoughts of the gods became a reality, so they were able to think up everything from the sky to the trees to the mountains. However, when the two gods find out that the creations they thought up were not able to praise them, they made others out of wood and clay. When these new beings caused some havoc on the whole world, then the two gods sent in a great flood in order to wipe them from existence and start from the beginning again.

In the second myth, the idea of creation was more of an awakening, with the darkness of the world turning into light through the actions of a man who was small and had a beard, known as the One Who Lives Above. The belief was that when this man rubbed his hands and face, he was able to create a few things like the Lightning Rumbler, Wind, Big Dipper, and the Sun god.

Then, these gods, through the help of a handshake, united, and the Creator was able to direct them to pull on a brown ball that he had dropped from his own hands in all of the directions in order to form the earth. With the help of the hummingbird, there were four cardinal points placed on the earth so that it would stay still.

The Hopi

Then we have the Hopi people and some of their legends. There are a few legends that come with this tribe, but one of the best ones is the Ant people, who were known for saving this tribe two separate times.

According to this tribe, the "First World" was originally destroyed because of fire (depending on the account it may have been from the sun, an eruption from a volcano or an asteroid striking the world). And then the "Second World was destroyed by ice thanks to the glaciers. In both of these worlds, the legend says that the tribe was guided by a cloud that was odd in shape, and then in the night, they were guided by a star that was moving. These guides then led them over to the sky god, who then took them over to the Ant People.

It was in some subterranean caves that these people were then able to find some refuge at the end of both the worlds in this legend, the Hopi people recognize the Ant People as generous and hard working. These people helped the Hopi to get food and taught them more about food storage when it was most needed.

One thing that is interesting here is that when we look to the Babylonian culture, they had a god of the sky named Anu. This was the word in Hopi for ant. Then Naki is the root word in Hopi for friends. So the ant friends in Hopi, or the Anu-Naki, could have been similar or the same as the Sumerian Annunaki as well, and this could provide us with some clues on where these people came from.

The Sioux

Sacred caves are also going to be important when it comes to the legends for the Sioux, especially when it comes to the location in South Dakota that is known as the Wind Cave National Park. In the Sioux legend, the Sioux feared one of the caves in that area, one that had wind that blew in and out of it. This was because they believed that there was a breathing giant who lived inside of it, and this giant was able to invoke the providence of their Great Spirit as well.

However, there is a slightly different legend because one of the medicine men who were curious is believed to have seen a new vision from a young maiden who told him she was the immortal buffalo lady who lived under the world. She then told this man to let the others know that this cave was a very sacred place, and the tribe was required to drop tokens and offerings there. This, in turn, would help them to find bigger herds of buffalo and see better results with their hunting expeditions.

The Lakota

The version of creation that the Lakota brings to us is going to begin off with some adultery. In this version of how the world started, the spider trickster, known as Inktomi, causes a bit rift between the Sun god and his wife, the Moon. This separation was enough to cause the time of day and night that we know now. While in the past, the gods had all been able to live in heaven, after this separation happened, Inktomi and the others who had helped him out where exiled to live on the Earth with the humans.

When he arrived, Inktomi then traveled underground in order to meet more about where humanity lived, and then convinced the first, or the Takahe, to come with them to the surface. He then comes out of the Wind Cave to find a place that is beautiful and then convinces some of the other families to head on up a well.

It doesn't take long for Takahe to figure out that he was tricked because the buffalo were scarce, the weather was not very good, and the families who had come p at the time were starving. To make things even worse, he, as well as the others who had come up with Inktomi, were not able to go back underground to their homes, and they had to spend the rest of their existence making it work on Earth instead.

The Cherokee

And we will end with a look at some of the myths that the Cherokee had about how the world originally began. In one of the myths, there was a great island that was able to float on the ocean, but it was attached to the sky by four ropes that were nice and thick. The sky was a rock. Because all around it was dark, the animals were not able to see anything.

This was when the Great Spirit came down and let the animals there know that they should stay awake for a total of seven days and seven nights. This was a long time to stay awake, and most of them were not able to do this. However, the plants which were able to do this found that they were able to stay green and lush all year long, and the animals who were able to remain awake through all that time, such as the mountain lion and the owl, were able to go and find their way in the dark as well

In a second story that the Cherokee have, everything in the world was water. Because there was nowhere for the animals to land to get a rest, the sky started to get overcrowded in no time. One day, there was a little water beetle who was named

Dayuni who was willing to go look underwater a bit in order to see what was there

This little water beetle fond some mud and then brought this mud back up to the surface with him. He brought back with him so much mud that eventually, he was able to create the Earth. As this mud and the Earth started to harden, they were able to pull out the sun that was hiding behind a rainbow and made sure it was up high in the sky to light up a path so everyone could see.

Without much of a doubt, the legends and stories about how the world began to vary depending on which tribe told them and even where they were located in the world. However, we are able to see that there are some links and similarities among the stories of all of them, no matter how far apart they each were, that can bring out some curiosities and questions about what may be found in the Earth and how it was able to create the world that we know more about in our modern world.

Keep in mind that many of these are going to focus on nature and the world that is around us, and many have animals associated with them as well. Unlike many of the modern religions that we use today, not all of the native tribes had a "creator" that they relied on to help bring about the beginning of the world, but they did have animals and a lot of nature. And humans always came after the animals had time to populate the world first. This gives us a unique perspective on what is found with the native tribes and what they hold most dear in their daily lives.

Art

Just like with all of the other topics we have explored in this chapter, the art of the native tribes varied quite a bit as well. Art has a very special part in the lives of these tribes ad it was often used as a way for the people to express themselves. Most arts were created as symbols, including people, eagles, walrus, and bears. The materials that were used for these pieces of art varied from fabric, clay cloth, feathers, and rocks.

Another type of artwork that was popular because it served more than one purpose was basket weaving. Cornhusks and reeds were woven in order to create these intricate baskets. Then the materials used could be dyed into some of the tribal patterns, which was able to result in a piece of art that would also be useful for transporting vegetables and fruits.

Many tribes would work with blanket weaving. Women could spend hours during the cold winter and even in the summer weaving the threads together in order to make a colorful blanket using the designs and patterns that were a big part of their culture. While many tribes are going to work with blankets for art, the Navajo tribe is one of the most known for some of the handwoven blankets they made.

In some of the northern regions where these native tribes lived, many would enjoy creating art as a kind of homage to their animal friends. For example, walruses were carved from the teeth of whales and bears, and eagles would be made out of rocks. Statues and some pendants were going to be created in order to show the respect that all of these tribes had for the animals

In addition to all of these, weapons and instruments were a form of art for many of these tribes, and all of these were made with care and lots of times. One of the most elaborate of the art forms for these tribes was the totem pole. These were huge, tall, and wooden that would be there to represent generations of family members for hat tribe or a particular family.

Each of the different faces on the totem pole would be a different kind of representation and could include the faces of people and animals. It was not uncommon for wings to come out of these poles as well. These poles were a very important part of all the culture of the Native American people, and we can find it spread out through many different tribes as well because it was a big part of their art culture at that time.

Chapter 7: Social Characteristics Tradition, Organization, Music, Handcrafts and Medicine of a Wise People

Tribal Organization

Another thing that we can focus on when it comes to these native tribes is their roles and organization within the tribe. No matter where the people lived, there was always a lot of work that they had to do just to survive. These people had to hunt, farm, find a way to prepare and store their food for the winter, build homes, make their clothing, and have some kind of protection against their enemies. For most of the societies, the work was divided up amongst the people with the women and men all performing some important work.

Although the roles and tasks were different based on the tribe and the region the people were in, you will find that in general, the way that the labor was divided up between the women and the men was similar for these tribes. The women would often take responsibility for the work that happened around the home like raising the children and cooking, and then the men were responsible for doing some of the work that was not in the home like raiding and hunting.

To start we will look at the work the women do. Women were in charge of the home, and sometimes, depending on their region, they would help out in the fields as well. Every person in the tribe had to pull their weight so we know women worked hard. Some of the tasks they needed to perform in order to help out includes:

1. Cooking: The women would cook and prepare meals. This could involve things like cleaning and skinning the animals gathering up nuts and fruits near the home, gathering some of the things in the fields preparing the food, smoking the meat so that it could be stored away safely for winter, and more.

2. Crafts: There was a lot of crafting skills that the women had that they were able to use around the home. They would prepare the animal hides to use in many cases. They could make clothing, weave cloth, and even make baskets in some cases.

3. Harvesting: In many of the tribes, the women would be responsible for harvesting the crops. There were times when the men would be there to help as

well, but this was often a task that the women would do.

4.   Other jobs: There were a number of other jobs that women had to do as well, including gathering up firewood and raising their children. When a tribe did move, it would be the responsibility of the women to help pack up the home and then get it all set up when they got back home.

The tasks that the women did no take care of would fall to the men as their responsibilities instead. Often these tasks would include things that would take the men away from home. Some of the tasks that were common for the men of a tribe to handle include:

1.   Hunting: The main job of the men would be to fish and hunt. Animals in these tribes were not just used as a food source. Often the skins of these animals would be used for clothing and to make the homes the people lived in.

2.   Fighting: Men were also held responsible for making war when it was needed and for protecting the whole village.

3.   Crafts: Most of the crafts that the men would engage in would have them working with their hands.

They could make weapons for hunting and some boats that they would use for traveling and fishing.

4.   Other jobs: For the most part, the men would be the religious and political leaders of the tribe. They often did the work that was hardest, such as helping to plant crops and build up the permanent homes that people would live in.

There are a few other important roles that we need to focus on when it comes to this society. First, there were many situations where men would work on other crafts, ones that were considered more detailed, like the ceremonial jewelry. The women would then be in charge of the homes. Unlike some of the western cultures of the time, the women would often be the ones who owned the home, along with everything that was inside of it, rather than the men.

In most tribes of the native people, the women were going to be well-respected because of their hard work and how they were able to provide food to their families. They were not seen as property or like they were less than the men, which was also a big change from what we see in many other cultures at the time. While the women and the men would have separate roles from one another, they would usually have equal rights. For example, while it was more common for the chief of a tribe to be a man, it was the women who were allowed to elect the chief an have a say in that.

Another unique thing to consider here is that today, about 25 percent of the tribes of Native Americans that are still around and that the federal government recognizes are led by women! This helps to show us just how valuable both genders were in the societies of these people, and how it was quite a bit different than some of the other ideas that were found in other cultures of the time.

Now that we know a bit about the different roles that men and women played at the time, we also need to explore more about some of the social structures of these tribes. This was so important to these societies, although there weren't any complex governments and rules that were written down. Despite this, there were defined social norms and structures that the people had to follow if they wanted to belong in the tribe.

When we look at the highest levels of these societies, we see the nations or the tribes. These were the large groups of people who shared a number of things in common, including their language, geography, and culture. Then in these tribes would be some smaller groups of the people known as the clan. The members of one clan would often have an ancestor in common and were more than likely related to one another. These clans would each have their spirit or symbol that provided their name.

Then we have the leaders of these tribes and clans who were known as the chiefs. These were men who were chosen or elected by the people they would look over. They would not usually have total power over everything, but they were men who were expected and who would provide advice that the clan or the tribe would follow.

In addition to the chief, there were many tribes who had a war leader as well as a civic leader. The civil leader was the one who guided the whole tribe when they were at peace, and then the war leader would be able to take over when the tribe was facing war with another nation.

From there, we are going to find that most clans were then divided up a bit more into families and villages. These groups were able to play a more important role in the lives of people on a day to day basis. It was not uncommon in these tribes for large and extended families to live with one another as well.

The forms of punishment that were used would change based on the tribe, but most of them would not include some kind of physical punishment to their members. Those who decided to go against the tribes or who did a crime would be rebuked and also shamed in front of the tribe. If the case got extreme enough, then these individuals would be taken out of the tribe.

The Native Americans were not that into material items and did not place value on these. There was not in the way of ownership and possessions, and people would not collect money in a bank or own land. They instead chose to value some intangible things like status, honor, and respect.

A few other things that we can consider the social structure that was found with many native tribes include:

1. Many of the early settlers called the chiefs of these tribes the kings.

2. Good deeds and being generous were things that the people respected more than possessions and wealth.

3. Membership in the clan was something determined by the mother of the child in some of the

tribes, but then others would do this based on the father of the child instead.

4.   The clan mother didn't have much power, but her opinion was one that others would listen to and respect.

5.   The religious leader was another important person in this society. They were often known as the Shaman or the medicine man.

Music

For many tribes, music was able to play a really important role in their lives. It was used to help with healing, for them to express themselves, recreation and fun, and even for some of their important ceremonies as well. There were a number of instruments that were used to make this music, including flutes and drums and a number of other percussion instruments. But the most important part of this music was the voice of the people.

Vocals were the backbone of the music that the native cultures were able to use, and when you listen to some of their music, you will be able to catch this quickly. Irregular rhythms that may be a bit unusual to what we are used to and a style of singing that was a bit off-key was often used. While some people would sing at once at times, harmony was not a bit part of this, and there were many solo performances that occurred as well.

Many of the tribes had vocals that were passionate, and the voices and words were used to invoke the spirits in some manner such as asking for healing or rain, and these songs could be used to help heal the sick. In many of the situations where music was used, the men and women of the tribe were able to sing their separate songs and their dances to go with that as well. It was common for men to dance around in a circle, and women were more likely to dance in place.

There are a lot of researchers who have come to the conclusion that the music the Native Americans used was some of the most complex that we are able to find in history. The tensing and then releasing of the vocals of tribes members combined with beats of the drum that often changed and varied made the whole music of these people an intricate art form.

Another item that we need to note here is that for all of the regions of the country that these tribes settled in, we are able to find a great variety of the sounds and forms of the music that they would create. This is part of the fun that we are able to find when it comes to listening to the music of these tribes. The music that is produced is always going to be unique to the specific group who produced it in the first place.

For the most part, the Eskimo music is known as the most simple of all the styles, and then the Zuni, Pueblo, and Hopi tribes tend to produce music that is more complex sounding than the others. Even though there isn't as much of this music produced today, the emotion that is found in this style has been a big influence that we can see in modern folk music.

Medicine

In our modern world, there are a lot of remedies out there to help us treat some of the more common ailments that we have. And often, these can be kind of harmful to us and our health, and many people are moving away from some of the traditional medicine over to some alternative therapies that will provide them with fewer side effects. Some of these can include the same medicines the Native Americans employed in the past.

The native people were around in Canada and the United States many years before all of the pharmaceuticals were around and before all of our modern prescription drugs. Because of this, these tribes were forced to rely on some natural remedies that came from the earth to help them to feel better from illness.

Many times the medicines that the native tribes had to rely on would be some combination of their magic, spirituality, and herbs. While it is common for a lot of modernists to balk against these methods to treat ailments, there are others who find that these practices are beneficial and can still work today. Often they work better than what our prescriptions can.

Each group of tribes has its unique approach to healing, so we can see some variation as we go through all of this. But you will notice that there are some similarities between Native American medicine and some of the approaches that the Chinese used. Both of these cultures value the treatment of the whole body, including the mind, spirit, and body. They don't want to just mask the issue; they want to work with natural elements to get to the core of the illness and cure it.

It was common for many of these tribes to have a medicine woman or man who would be responsible for performing all of his healing. These were their versions of doctors. Before they would treat one of the patients, the medicine person in the tribe would need to fully understand the condition they were treating. Then they would be able to work a variety of rituals and herbs in order to treat these different ailments.

After the medicine person knew more about the problem they were trying to solve, they would then be able to administer the herb medicine that was meant to cure that problem. In some cases, based on what was wrong, the doctor would then recommend some kind of ritual purification. The point of doing this was to help rid the body of some harmful toxins that may have been causing that particular health problem at the time.

There were also a few haling practices that the Native Americans were able to rely on as well. To start, the powwow was a combination of the sacred and the social coming together of these people. There would be an arena in the shape of a circle where the tribe people would dance, sing, and rum. Many of those who showed up here would wear their traditional regalia, and they usually would fashion and design on their own.

Wearing this regalia and then dancing around the arena circle is show solidarity with the identities they had as Native Americans, and they would give expression and meaning to these terms like "we are all related" in the Lakota language. Those who attend the powwow often have some individualized experience. In addition to the drumming and all of the dancing, there will be some trade booths around to share with other goods, musical instruments, foods, crafts, and foods.

Another option is to work with the pipe ceremony. According to one of the traditions of the Lakota people, one person named White Buffalo Cow Woman brought what is known as the sacred pipe to the Lakota people and a few other of their sacraments as well. The bowl for the pipe was made out of red catlinite, while the stem was going to be made from some hardware instead.

The stem and the pipe are going to be separated from one another except when it is time to use them in the ceremony. Common tobacco was not something used in this ritual, and it would be a mixture of different herbs like sage and red willow. Tobacco was not something that was meant for inhalation pleasure, but instead, it is meant to help carry up the prayers of the people to their Creator.

The pipe ceremony would often happen along with some of the other religious ceremonies of these tribes, including the inipi When using the pipe; those participating would either sit or stand in the circle and could pass the pipe from one of them to another, taking the time to pray and smoke it as it went. Many participants used this as a way to pray or to gather up some relief and peace after something bad had happened in their lives

Many times the traditional Native Americans would observe the various plants in their environment and would learn more about which parts of different plants could help them with healing. By the time the Europeans landed on this continent, the Native Americans had experienced a good health level from the herbal treatments and some of their more traditional diets.

Unlike what was found in western medicine, it is believed that the health benefits and more that came from the medicines were not solely from the herbs on their own but the healthy lifestyle and the spiritual connection that the healer has with the plants is important as well. This is a big reason why the prescription and over the counter medicines that we use today are not going to be the equivalent and won't provide us with the same benefits.

One unique view that was given during this time is that the healers thought that the herbs were one of the means to help bring back some more balance for an individual. This balance could be in many different dimensions, including spiritual, intellectual, and emotional, while also helping with the physical. All the other aspects had to be taken care of as well and then the herbs could do more of their work in all of this.

The Native Americans lived a lifestyle that is quite a bit different than what we see in our modern western world. And there are many people who believe that this was important to how well they were able to survive without many illnesses for many years and in the harmony that the native people had to the land around the Their medicine, their artwork, their way of life and everything else around them all helped to shape the various unique cultures that these native tribes enjoyed.

Chapter 8
Environment, Nature, and Earth
The Current Teachings
of an Ancient People

Another topic that we need to spend some time on is looking at how the native tribes, even when they are completely different and found in different parts of the continent, are going to value and appreciate the Earth, nature, and the environment. This is a big difference from what many of us are going to know and be used to in our modern world. But this doesn't mean that we are not able to learn about all of these things and learn how to focus on the good in nature and a balance between all of the parts, along the way as well. Let's take a look at some of the common views that the native people have about the earth, nature, and the environment and see what we are able to learn more in the process.

Indian Aphorisms

There are many thoughts that the Native Americans are going to focus on to help remind us about the importance of nature and how we are able to live in harmony with all that is around us, whether it is nature, the animals which surround us, and so much more. Each of the major tribes will show us that this harmony with nature is going to be so important to helping us get the results that we want, and can give us a life that is wholesome and not bad for us.

To start, we can look at the quote from Big Thunder, an Algonquin leader. He explains that the Great Spirit can be found in all things. This Great Spirit is found in the air that we need to breathe and is considered the Father of the world. But, the Earth is important as well, because she is our Mother, the one who is responsible for nourishing us. When we take care of the earth, everything that we put into the ground is going to be returned thanks to Earth.

According to Black Elk who was part of the Oglala Sioux tribe, "The first piece which is going to be the most important, is that which comes within the souls of people when they realize their relationship their oneness with the Universe and all its powers and when they realize that at the center of the Universe dwells the Great Spirit and that this center is everywhere it is within each of us.

In the next one, we are able to take a look at one of the proverbs that are shared by the Cree Indians. In this one, we can remember the following "Only when the last tree has died, and the last river has been poisoned, and the last fish been caught will we realize that we cannot eat money." This helps us to see how much the native tribes respected the earth. They knew that if they did not take care of the resources they had now, then soon it would be all gone and they would not be able to survive any longer.

Then we can move on to another option of an ancient proverb of the native people. With this one, it reminds us that we are not the ones who own the land and that it was not something that was handed down to us by our parents. Instead, they encourage us to remember that this land was something that we loan out from our children because we are not going to inherit the Earth and all that is in from those in the past, but instead, we are going to borrow it from our children.

Another thought that we could hold onto when it comes to working with nature, environment, and Earth and how the native people worked with all of these is going to come to us from Chief Seattle. This quote says, "Humankind has not woven the web of life. We are but one thread within it. Whatever we do to the web, we do to ourselves. All things are bound together. All things connect."

Then there are some thoughts that we can take a look at when it comes to the Sioux Lakota people through John Lame Deer. He states that before the white people came to their land, and worked to make the native people into more civilized people, there weren't any prisons in this culture. And because of this, there weren't any delinquents at all. Without a prison, there can be no delinquents.

Going along with this, he states that the people did not have keys or locks on their belongings, and they didn't have thieves to worry about. When there was someone who didn't have the money in order to get a blanket or a tent or a horse, then the tribes would take care of them and provide these things. The people of these tribes were not valued by their wealth and they were taken more as who they were rather than what they had and because of this, there weren't any laws that they had to write down and there were no ideas like politicians or lawyers and them were not interested or even able to swindle and cheat one another at all.

And finally, John Lame Deer talked about how they were not in that bad of shape before the white people came and told them the natives were doing things in the wrong manner. They thought that they got along well, they didn't have to worry about prison or people stealing, and if something happened and you did not have money, someone would take care of you. It seems like a much better life to live than what we see with a lot of the common modern ways that we have it, and it includes living in harmony with those around you ad with nature as well.

We can also take a look at some of the more religious options that we can focus on when it is time to work with the native tribes. They had a different way of handling a lot of the things that we need to focus on, rather than worrying or going towards our modern trappings, and even some of the more ancient tribes were able to help us out with some of these things as well.

According to one of the chiefs who are unknown right now, "Peace and happiness are available at every moment. Peace is every step. We shall walk hand in hand. There are no political solutions to spiritual problems. Remember, if the Creator put it there, it is in the right place. The soul would have no rainbow if the eyes had no tears. Tell your people that, since we were promised we should never be moved, we have been moved five times.

As we can see, with many of the thoughts and the quotes that we are able to find here, the native people were all about being in connection with not only one another, but also with nature, the animals, and everything that was around them. These need to come together in order to make sure that we are going to end up with a happy and healthy life, and to make sure that all of our resources and the life we enjoy will be around not only for us but also for all of the other people who come after us as well.

This is a big contrast to what we see in our modern world. We are part of the culture of taking in more, and using more, often more than what we need at any given time. This is wasteful and against a lot of what the native people would recommend for us to work with. But it is also causing us a lot of trouble and leaves us with a life that is not all that good and healthy for us.

We can learn a bit more about how native people treat nature and the things around them. This is something that we are able to focus on in order to improve our own lives.

Think about how much things could change if we focused more on what the balance between nature and ourselves could be if we tried a bit.

Respect for Mother Nature and the Earth

There are a lot of ways that the native people were able to show their respect for mother nature and the earth. They lived in harmony with the world around them and were able to do this for many thousands of years without much of a difference on the landscape around them. One of the ways that they were able to show how much they respected and valued the earth around them was in their stories. While there are many native legends that are fun to look at we are going to take a look at some of the ones that best show us the way that the natives valued nature:

Brother Buffalo and Brother Crow

At the beginning of time, the crow was pure white. He was considered the brother of the great buffalo. The Shawnee people in that area relied on buffalo for their skins and food, but each time that the Shawnee tried to do a hunt on the buffalo, the crow would find out and tell him.

During this time, the hunting party would gather around their evening campfire to prepare a hunt. Cawanemua talked first and said, "We need to do something about the crow. I will hide as a buffalo, and when brother crow comes out to warn of our hunt, I can grab him and stop him."

And the next day, this is exactly what Cawanemua did. He pulled a big skin of buffalo over him and then joined the herd that was grazing by the camp. Before long, the crow came by to warn of some Shawnee hunters who were approaching. This is when Cawanemau jumped out of the skin, caught the crow, and carried him all the way back to the camp.

For that night a the fire, the hunters tried to discuss what would have to the crow. The smallest brave, known as Panseau, listened in on the conversation and also was responsible for watching the crow. Some in the party wanted to just kill and then eat the crow because they were hungry, and the crow was responsible for that. Others were happy to let the crow go, believing that the crow had learned a lesson and would not go and warn the buffalos again.

At this time, Cawanemau was getting angry, and he decided to grab up the crow and throw him in the first. Panseau, who was noticing that the crow was turning black from all the soot in the soot inside of the fire, took the crow up from the flames. This made Cawanemau even more furious and he yelled, "Why would you help the crow? We are all going cold and hungry because of what he has done, but you still save him out of the flames of the fire!"

In a small voice, Panseau simply said, "The crow warns his brother. That is the same that I would do for you, my brother.

The crow was shaken from the flames and was blackened as well. It was silent for a moment as everyone considered what the young warrior had said. Then the crow stated, "I am blackened because I warned the buffalo, who is my brother, and I wanted to protect. Now I saw that the Shawnee people are y brother as well. I will no longer warn the buffalo of your future hunts, as long as you remember to always give thanks to the buffalo for giving himself as your food and clothing."

This is when Cawanemau stood up and said, "The Crow is now our brother, and so is the buffalo. We will only go on a hunt for the buffalo when we are in need of food and skins, and nothing else. And we promise to give thanks after each hunt. Our new brother crow must remain black as this will help him to remember this pledge, and as a reminder to us as well."

Resource Approach

The native people were good at managing their resources and being in harmony with the world around them. They knew that the resources they were using were finite, and if something went wrong and one died out, they would be the ones to suffer as well. If they were wasteful and didn't take care of the animals and more around them, then there was no way that the people and the tribes would be able to survive for a very long time either

The kinds of foods that these tribes ate, the clothing they were able to wore, and even their homes would depend on the seasons. The foods they were able to eat changed with the seasons as well. for example, in the winter, they would live on the foods they stored in the fall and hunted for some animals and birds when possible. In the sprint, they would fish, pick berries, and hunt. When the summer finally came, they would grow some crops. And then they would finish it out in the fall by hunting for food and harvesting crops that they could then preserve to get them through the winter.

The native tribes were able to use these natural resources in every aspect of their lives. The skins would be used as clothing, and the shelter was made from branches, animal furs and other materials that are around them. These native people would also fish, hunt, and farm and would use any of the natural resources they could find in order to accomplish this.

Indian men were primarily the ones who would do the hunting and the fishing. Each winter, the men in the various tribes would come together to work on their expeditions, making it more efficient and ensuring that they would only take the amount that they need. The deer meat would be a good supplement to a diet that relied mainly on agriculture at the time. Even after the hunt, the Indians would not just rely on the meat, choosing to make good use of their resources and sing the skin of the animals for their clothing and the bones as some of their tools as well.

Unlike many of the settlers who were coming into the land, the Indians valued Mather Nature and all that she would provide for them. They learned to just take what they needed and nothing more, choosing to keep the balance and the harmony of the earth intact, or they knew it could spell some consequences for them if they were not able to do this. The Indians were a part of this balance as well and believed that it was good for them to hunt and use the materials around them, as long as it was done in a responsible manner.

Often before some of these expeditions, the tribes would come together and perform some of their spiritual traditions to help with the hunt. They would ask the spirits to bless their hunt and to protect them, and then when it was done, they would be thankful and perform rituals as well. This helped the people to remember what they were doing, how to be mindful about what they used, and so much more.

When hunting or fishing was done all of the parts would be done in order to prevent as much waste as possible. The fur, the skin, the bones, and all the parts possible were used to help the native tribes handle some of their daily requirements like clothing, homes, tools, weapons, and more. This helped them to maintain the balance that nature needed and could help them to have more for later.

The native people loved and respected the world that was around them at all times. They knew that this was part of their lives and that they should be thankful for some of the experiences and chances that they were able to get from the earth, and that they should cherish and respect it. This helped to change and form a lot of the customs and more that they used in their daily lives.

We in our modern world could learn some valuable tips and more about how to treat the world around us. Instead of using up all of our resources and being more wasteful in the way that we treat our food, our clothes, and other things that we implement into our daily lives as well.

Chapter 9
After the Wars Until Now

We spent some time in an earlier part of this book takes a look at all of the wars that happened with the native people and how the white settlers continued to go west and push the native people farther and farther out of their lands. While many of the Native Americans worked hard to try and stay in their lands and many tried to fight, with a few who were successful, after some time, the U.S. government won, and the Indians had to give up and give in.

This was not necessarily a good time for the native people. There were a lot of hardships that happened for them and even though there were some protests and more along the way. Let's take a closer look at some of the things that happened to the various native tribes after the wards and how this would forever change the culture and the lives of these people.

Sterilization Campaigns

The first thing that we are going to focus on is the idea of the sterilization campaigns that happened against the native people. Between the years of 1907 to 1939, about 30,000 people in our country were sterilized. Some of these were against their will and others did not know until it was too late. But this continued to go on for a long time afterward. In fact, in the 1960s and 70s, it is estimated that the US Indian Health Service forced sterilization on women with Native American backgrounds, and about 3,406 of these happened between the years of 1973 to 1976.

It was then in 1876 wen the General Accounting Office then admitted that this happened in a minimum of four of the 12 Indian Health Service regions and it was believed that at least 36 of these women were young, falling under the age of 21, even though there were court orders that forbade this procedure being done on anyone who wasn't over that age. The study that brought some of this to light was limited and underfunded, and it is believed that the actual numbers of Native Americans who have been sterilized through the years could be a lot higher.

In another study that was done in 1974, Dr. Connie Pinkerton-Uri, a physician with Cherokee and Chocktaw heritage, found that about 25 percent of the American Indian women were sterilized and none of them had provided consent to do this. The conclusion from this is that the Indian Health Services, which was supposed to be on the side of the Native American and who was supposed to provide them with the health and care they needed, were singling out Indian women, especially those who were full-blooded, for these procedures.

Some experts in this estimate that about half of the women of Native American heritage were sterilized and that the age of these women was not old enough to consider this as a healthy option. Most of the women who went through this were somewhere between the age of 15 to 44, and many were too young to get the procedure at all, whether they agreed to it or not.

This had some dramatic negative effects on the native populations. With the population of Native Americans at 1 million in 1976, this process of sterilization was going to cause the survival of the tribe to go way down. It is estimated that there are only around 100,000 Native American women at the age of childbearing left. While a population with 200 million could support some form of voluntary sterilization and they would be fie, but with the lower numbers of Native Americans, this could not be the choice of birth control at all. When the Native American people are gone, they can't come back, and we can't find ancestors of theirs in other regions of the world.

So, why did this happen? And why was it done on an estimated 50 percent of the women in these tribes? There is believed to be some combination of factors, including social, racial, and economical. To start, the war on poverty in the 1960s, there was a huge increase in how many people were on the welfare program. According to a study done in 1973 by the Health Research Group, and other interviews that happened in the years after most physicians who performed this non-voluntary sterilization happened to be males, who were white, who believed that they were helping out the country when they could limit how many births these lower-minority families could have.

With this mindset, the physicians were working with the mindset that they were enabling a way for the government to cut down on some of the funding of the welfare and the Medicaid programs while also being able to reduce their tax burden and how much they had to put in each year to support these federal programs for the minorities who had a lot of children.

There was also an economic incentive that showed up. They were able to increase their income when they did things like tubal ligations and hysterectomies rather than providing birth control; some of them did not think that minority women, including the Native American, would be capable of effectively working with other forms of birth control at all.

This was also a time when there was a huge amount of social protest by various organizations of Native Americans and African Americans. These groups were seen by the whites around them as dangerous, radical, and militant, and this made the doctors more eager to sterilize women in these minority groups. Other doctors were more interested in gaining some experience in the OBGYN field, and they would work with minority women, often without permission, to get that experience on the government dime.

Then there were the medical personnel who believed that they were there helping out all of these women. They thought that with fewer children, these minority families could then be more secure financially while also lessening the welfare burden on others.

Of course, we know that this process of sterilization was affecting women and their families and the communities that they were in. It was common for marriage to dissolve in the process, and these women were more likely to suffer high rates of psychological problems along the way, including dealing with feelings of guilt and shame, alcoholism and drug abuse.

It is often believed that while other minority groups had similar stories, the Native American woman was more at risk because they were socially invisible, with smaller numbers, and they were able to get away with this more without others having any idea. It took a long time, and lots of interviews with the women affected, investigative analyses, news reports, and even hearings before some of the negativity were brought to light and we were able to see more about the scope on how these forced sterilizations affected the tribe, the family, and the individual.

Reserves

We talked about these reserves a bit in the rest of the book, but it is important to know a bit more about these and what they did to the Native Americans. This reserve system was meant to establish tracts of land for the natives to live on while the settlers were able to take over the other land. The main goal was to make sure that the native tribes would be under the control of the U.S. government and to help minimize the amount of conflict that the settlers and Indians had to face.

While this may have sounded good on the surface, there were a lot of drawbacks to this in the process, and it completely benefited the white settlers. Many of these tribes were forced onto the reservations and it brought some horrible results that we are still able to notice today.

Daily life on the reservations was not easy and often hard. Not only were the tribes kicked off of their native lands, but they found that maintaining their traditions and cultures in the confined areas of the reservations was pretty much impossible.

It was also common for tribes that did not get along and who were feuding on a regular basis to be thrown together. And many of the hunter tribes of the past were forced to become farmers to survive. It was common for many on the reservations to starve, and living in the close quarters was able to hasten up the spread of many diseases that white settlers had brought over in the first place

Part of this was to encourage the Indians to become white and assimilate, and many times these tribes were forced and encouraged to wear non-Indian clothes while learning to write and read in English. They were also there to learn how to raise livestock and to sew like the whites. There were often many missionaries who came in and attempted to convert these people over to Christianity in order to change up the spiritual beliefs.

Then in 1887, things got more complicated. This was when President Grover Cleveland signed in the Dawes Act, which allowed the government to take the reservations and divide it up into some smaller plots of land that the individual Indians could have. The hope with this one was that the Indians would then find it easier to assimilate into the white culture while also improving their quality of life.

Even if it was meant to help, this act was enough to cause a devastating impact on these native tribes. It decreased the amount of land that these Indians owned by half and allowed the railroad and other white settlers to have even more land. And most of the land that was left for the reservations weren't good enough to farm. Add to this that the people were not able to afford the tools and supplies to start farming, and it just made things worse.

Before this reservation system was put into place, the women of the tribes would farm and take care of the land so that the men had time to protect the tribe and hunt. Now, the men were forced to change up and start with the farming, something they were not used to handling, and the women were able to take on roles that were more domestic in the process

After a review of the life of how Indians were living on the reservations, which is known as the Meriam Survey, it was very easy to see that the Dawes Act was detrimental to these tribes. It was ended in 1934 an replaced with something known as the Indian Reorganization Act. This was an act that had the goal of restoring the culture to the Indian tribes and returning some of the surplus lands as well. it also allowed for the tribes to be able to self-govern and write out their constitutions at the time while providing financial aid to these tribes as they grew again.

The modern reservations are still found throughout the United States, and they are governed and watched out for by the Bureau of Indian Affairs. The tribes who are on these reservations are sovereign and they are not forced to follow any of the federal laws that are in place. They are able to handle most of the obligations of the reservation but often, they are so small that they rely on financial aid from the government. On many of the reservations that are more self-sufficient, they rely on gambling and tourism to make it through.

It is estimated by the BIA that there are 567 Native tribes in the United States. And it is the job of the BIA in order to improve the quality of life of these people, providing them with some opportunities economically, and help them to improve their assets, which the BIA is going to hold in trust right now.

Even with some of these efforts, living conditions that are found on these reservations are still not that ideal, and they are compared in many cases to what is found in a third world country. The housing available is crowded to the extreme and doesn't often meet quality standards. And many people who are on these reservations find that they are stuck in poverty as they go through.

The health care that these individuals receive will be provided through the Indian Health Services, but it is something that is not funded the best, and there are some areas where this is not even possible. There are a lot of Native Americans who are going to die from diseases like diabetes and heart disease because of their lifestyle choices. The infant mortality rates are a bit higher than what we see with whites, and it is estimated that drug abuse and alcohol are on the rise. Many people leave these areas to go into urban areas to find better work and better living conditions.

The reservation of the Indians was established in the first place as a result of many prejudice and greed of the early settlers in America, and the federal government who used force in order to make the natives behave in the manner that they wanted. Despite all of the challenges that have happened in the past and today, these Native American people continue to hold onto all of the heritage of the past, and they thrive as a community as well.

Indian Protests

While most of the native tribes had to take a step back and give in to what the federal government wanted because they did not have the people or the resources in order to keep fighting, there have still been a lot of protests and activism by this group of people for some of the things that they think is important to them. We are going to take a look at how these work and how the native people were able to get their voices heard:

1.   The Modoc War (1872 to 1873): This is going to be known in many cases as the Lava Beds War. This is where 150 members of the Modoc tribe worked together to resist the U.S> Army for months to hold onto their strategic positions that were near Tule Lake. In the end, their leader was tried for various war crimes because he sent two army representatives who were sent to help negotiate peace there. He was later hanged, and the rest of the followers were held in Oklahoma as prisoners of war.

2.   Occupation of Alcatraz: With this one, there were 89 Native Americans who spent 19 months occupying the Alcatraz Island. They were eventually

removed thanks to the forces of the government. Then the IOAT or the Indians of All Tribes claimed rights to that island thanks to the Treaty of Fort Laramie, which was supposed to return all of the abandoned, unused, ore retired lands of the government back to the native people who used to own it.

3. Chicago in 1971: In this one, the Native Americans were able to set up what was known as a community of occupation near Wrigley Field. There were around 30 native people who took part in this demonstration. Their goal was to call attention over to the inferior housing that most indigenous people in the Chicago area had to deal with.

4. Nike Missile Facility in 1971: After the occupation that had occurred at Alcatraz, there was a smaller group of these activists who tried to take over control of what was known as the Nike Missile facility in Richmond, California. In the past few years, the site had been left and fallen into disrepair. The IOAT members claimed that they were the ones who owned this because they should have gotten the land back with the government not using it.

5.   Milwaukee in 1971: IN this one, there were about 25 people who belonged to the AIM, or the American Indian Movement, who worked together to take over the U.S> Coast Guard station that had been abandoned at that time. The activists were using the same logic as what had been used with some of the other protests in order to take over that area as their own.

6.   The 1972 takeover of the BIA: During November of this time, there were about 500 native Americans who occupied the BIA building in the D.C. area. They had been able to travel to Washington in order to raise some more awareness about how bad the housing situation was on the reservations for their people. After about a week, they all disbanded, taking the time to remove or otherwise destroy some of the government records on land deeds, treaties, and water rights

7.   1973 incident at Wounded Knee: There were about 200 AM members as well as tribe members of Lakota who were able to seize the town of Wounded Knee, which was found on the Pine Ridge reservation

in the South Dakota area. They demanded that all of the negotiations on treaties would reopen and the removal of the current tribal president of Richard Wilson. This ended up in a big standoff as well with the U.S. marshals and FBI. This lasted for about 71 days, during which the back and forth shooting was frequent, and there were two activists who were killed.

These are just a few of the protests that the native people tried to do against the government and others who did not understand their plight at all. This was a strong people, ones who have never given up on what they believed in and did not always conform to what others, including the government and the white people, wanted of them. And because of this, and the fact that they tried to go through and learn how to keep their lands and their traditions, there have been a number of skirmishes that have shown up over the years, including some of the ones that we talked about above.

Assimilation and Integration

Through all of the methods that were talked about in this guidebook, we can find that the whole goal, along with being prejudiced and not liking these tribes, is that the whites wanted to force these tribe members to assimilate and integrate into the way that the whites wanted.

The settlers and the governments did not want to learn about the various religious and spiritual ways of the native people. They didn't want to learn about the artwork, the music, the culture, the language, or anything else about the Indians. They mostly thought that this was a bad culture and that the Indian people were seen as savages along the way. And this gave them some of the justification that was necessary to do some of the things that they did along the way

Instead of learning from and embracing some of the different parts that come with the native people, the whites wanted to make them assimilate and integrate into their society. The reservations and all of the other options were there to ensure that the Indians would give up their ways and start to fit into what was considered normal by the white people. They had to learn English. They had to give up some of their traditional outfits and start to wear the same clothes as the whites. They had to learn how to work and farm like the white people, how to follow the same customs, and they were even required to go through and change religions as well.

There wasn't room, at least in the minds of the whites, for the white culture and the culture of the Native Americans at all. There was only one right manner of living, and the whites would only accept that their way was the right way. And this is why much of the history and the traditions and more of the Indians were wiped out, and many of these people are still struggling to find their place and hold onto their way of life even in some of our modern world as well.

The plight of the Native American. While they were able to live simply and harmoniously for many years before the white people came, once these settlers brought their new ideas and a new way of living to the native people, all started to go downhill. There have always been individuals and tribes who tried to fight against the white people and the injustices, and there are still those who try to stand up for better living conditions and wages and more for the people, there is still a lot of work that has to be done.

Understanding more about how these people lived, what they went through, what they believed in, and more was so important to helping them to live on and for helping them to maintain their culture. It has not been easy on any of the tribes since the white man showed up, and it still is not that easy for them at all. But we can do well to remember these people, how they lived in harmony for many years, and how strong in faith and their traditions they can be.

Conclusion

Thank you for making it through to the end of *Respect the Earth and Love the Land*, let's hope it was informative and able to provide you with all of the tools you need to achieve your goals whatever they may be.

The Native American people had a unique kind of culture that was not found in any other part of the world, and one that was able to last for thousands of years before the whites showed up. Their integration with and the respect that they had for our natural world meant that for all of this time, they had the ability to live in great harmony with the landscapes they found themselves in, no matter what that landscape was all about. They produced just enough to meet the needs they had and didn't take advantage of it or throw nature out of balance. This is something that can make some of their philosophies so interesting to us in our modern times, in a time when humans struggle with how much they impact the planet.

However, because of the simplicity of the lives of these tribes, it meant that they had a lot of trouble resisting the appearance of those from Europe, those who brought new technologies and ideas with them. The Native Americans of this time period lived a life that was very different compared to those of their ancestors thanks to the Europeans. Against military tactics and modern weapons, they didn't have a good advantage here.

When all of this was combined with some of the devastations that the diseases took on these people thanks to the European and the sudden discovery of the distilled liquors, many of the societies and cultures that were here for a long period of time were suddenly gone in just a few years.

The victory of the United States and how well it did in the Revolutionary War meant that there wasn't going to be any kind of consideration and no mercy for the people that were considered savages by the Americans. These natives were taken out of their lands and even restricted to areas that were so bad that most were not able to make a living for themselves at all.

In other places, they were hunted down and killed or treated just like wild animals. And the native people did not fare well in any of these conditions. Even when treaties were reached, many times, they were not very good for the natives, and most of them were ignored as soon as it became beneficial for the government to do so.

There are still a lot of lessons that we are able to learn from the native people, even though many of them are gone today, and the ones left are often on reservations and not living the life of their ancestors at all. We can learn how to better treat those around us, even those who are different. We can learn to appreciate what we have formed the land, and not take too much or use up our limited resources along the way. And we can love some of the traditions and spiritual journeys in a way that is similar to these people as well.

Finally, if you found this book useful in any way, a review on Amazon is always appreciated!